Call Her by Her Name

Bianca Lynne Spriggs

Call Her by Her Name

Poems

TRIQUARTERLY BOOKS/NORTHWESTERN UNIVERSITY PRESS

EVANSTON, ILLINOIS

TriQuarterly Books
Northwestern University Press
www.nupress.northwestern.edu

Printed in the United States of America

10 9 8 7 6 5 4 3 2 1

Library of Congress Cataloging-in-Publication Data

Names: Spriggs, Bianca Lynne, author.
Title: Call her by her name : poems / Bianca Lynne Spriggs.
Description: Evanston, Illinois : TriQuarterly Books/Northwestern University Press, 2016. |
    Includes bibliographical references.
Identifiers: LCCN 2016001856 | ISBN 9780810132764 (pbk. : alk. paper) |
    ISBN 9780810132771 (e-book)
Classification: LCC PS3619.P744 C35 2016 | DDC 811.6—dc23
LC record available at http://lccn.loc.gov/2016001856

The paper used in this publication meets the minimum requirements of the American
National Standard for Information Sciences—Permanence of Paper for Printed Library
Materials, ANSI Z39.48–1992.

for the women

CONTENTS

. . . is not the lute that soothes your spirit
the very wood that was hollowed with knives?

—KHALIL GIBRAN

Pedicure

No one remembers your feet.
I cannot let you be buried
in ashy ankles and flecked paint.

Never could figure out why you liked
your polish in shades of bruise:
eggplant, navy, hunter green.

You so hated people touching your toes,
hated anyone else's coming near you.
I balance on the wheeled stool—get to work

on your left one first, lifting your patent black flat
and rolling down the sheer dress sock, slow—slow.
Your heel feels too light and I half expect

you to wake up, yank it away complaining
how your sole is ticklish—you don't.
So I get the right one ready too. Patent flat off.

Sheer sock off. Your toes are a mess.
What is left of a shade that might have once
been mocha, mottles your toenails.

I pull the remover and cotton balls from my purse
and get to rubbing away the polish one toe at a time.
Your ankles, smooth, dry; the flesh—cracked.

I have a vial of our mother's blessed oil left
to rub into them. And I do—seal the rifts
in your skin with olive oil and gold flakes,

myrrh and her prayers. It is too quiet, too cold.
I imagine if it was just us, really us, and not Death
too, there would be music—I start singing

but the only song that comes to mind is by Frankie Valli
and I hope you're somewhere laughing at me,
picking up the chorus I've dropped all over the floor.

When you are clean, I pull out a platinum
polish called, *mithril*. You were always
a little bit razor blade, a little bit shooting star.

The polish shines like nothing could chip it,
not a jackhammer, not some hero's mythic blade.
I finish the first and begin a second coat,

getting into it now, the back and forth
of the little brush coloring in your nail; I forget
that your skin feels like the outside of an ice cooler.

And this is my last memory of us: me, you,
Frankie Valli, and your bony, yella', size-eleven feet—
I lean forward and begin to blow.

Introducing

The girls next door peek through
faded pink bedroom sheets
they have fashioned into temporary
window curtains. When I walk past,
one of them calls,

Hey, woman!

The other squeals,
sheets fluttering into the wings
of an immense cotton butterfly
on the cusp of flight.

I like your whole outfit!

I smile up, *Thank you!*
Another flurry of fabric
and chirruping voices,
two sets of huge brown eyes
and frizzy pigtails.
This is a wonderful new game—
talking to this strange, quiet
woman next door.

Hi!

Hi!

Hi, woman!

High girls roosting
in their second-story
tower recover a memory.

What did she and I do on a day
that was all drizzle and mist
when our parents weren't home
on a Saturday afternoon?
What did we do before
the whole family collided again
after errands and housework,
everyone grouped in the living room
over carryout and lap trays
around reruns of *Star Trek*,
my sister, picky eater,
neglecting her food to play
with bows and brushes
in our father's hair.
I seem to remember bouts
of "Introducing!," my favorite game,
where someone's bed served
as a stage and whichever of us
wasn't on, had to settle for announcer,
and drum roll with her tongue,
and call out with much excitement,

     Introducing _____!

followed by the other's full name.
And then the performer whipped
up a song or a story that involved much
jumping and gyration, a prized toy,
and outdoing whomever was singing
on our ladybug record player.

I seem to remember too
when our parents were home
and sometimes it wasn't raining,
but I kept my sister in her room anyway
with the music all the way up,
doing my best to outshout my father
whose cursing and slamming doors
could be felt across the house.

     Introduce me!
     It's my turn!
     Introduce me!

My sister loved to bounce on her bed,
which she would later slide off
in the middle of the night
to sleep halfway standing up,
thumb in her mouth, death-grip
on Pink Bear, who ended up
the same washed-out pink
as the girls' bed sheets fluttering
above the street next door.

     It's my turn!
     My! Turn!

Arguing ensues
over whose turn it *really* is—
and by now the girls next door
have long forgotten all about me.

The Skate Doctor

It is summer in Lake Worth. I am eight
and need new bearings for the wheels
of my high-booted dance skates.

My father brings me to see the skate doctor
in his ten-by-ten storage unit workshop.

My skin is still freshly painted. Five bucks
at the Palace skating rink gets you a full face
of cursive brushstrokes and a little glitter.

War paint for the Saturday races.
Even as teal and white illuminate my eyes,

I see sparkles at the edges of my vision.
I tell the skate doctor I am ready for more
speed as he smokes over my skates.

His voice is lost forever to memory, but not his
plexiglass-thick spectacles or friartuck haircut.

He gestures to a crate—his coffee table—stained
with axel grease, covered in cigarette butts.
There, the image of my first pair of racing quads

waits in the center of a dog-eared catalog.
Mine would have hot-pink laces. Wheels to match.

Clipped newsprint photos peel from the walls,
wave like palms away from a slow-ticking floor fan.
Trophies tall as me—saplings—sprout

from the concrete. When was he ever anything
but this old gnome, growling over a pair

of child's skates, arthritic knuckles that bulge
with each wrench—he murmurs
that if I want to learn how to fly on wheels,

I've come to the right place.

Recess: A Bop

Mami Wata is in my kitchen and we are playin'
all her favorite hand-clap games. This is the first
time I've not gone sleep-walkin' to find her
in some midnight river or stream. She's here
cloaked in jade and lilac, poppin' her gum
and crackin' on me and my taste in men.

Sittin' in a native hut
All alone and blue
Sittin' in a native hut
Wonderin' what to do

Mami Wata grabs a palm, and just like my best
grade-school girlfriend reads my love line
aloud like it is poetry. We've gone through
two bottles of champagne and now we need
fruit and pound cake and chocolate wrapped
in thin gold foil. She means to dance and starts
off with a slow buck step before shakin'
her limbs out into wings.

Along came a native girl
Did a native dance
It was like in paradise
Put me in a trance

Mami Wata is grindin' barefoot on a Tuesday
in my kitchen, python slung low 'round her hips.

She stomps the dust free from the windowpanes
before leavin' to shimmy on out the back door
toward wherever her next horizon might be—
the only direction she knows best.

Shimmy shimmy ko-ko bop
Shimmy shimmy bop
You can do the ko-ko bop
Now's no time to stop

the Other Left

Emma holds her left hand in an L,
closes her eyes, tries to imagine
the map facing another direction.
She turns the map upside down.
That's better. She only meant to stop
in this parking lot for a few minutes.
Long enough to reorient.
Long enough to get a coffee, be on her way.
But she only knows one way out of this town.
The other routes have slits for eyes.
She thought she was heading
toward the highway when she realized
a circle kept bringing her back.
So she stops. Asks the clouds for a sign.
Looks down and sees a face she knows.
She went to school with the woman
stepping into the silver sedan.
She remembers passing her in the hallways.
Sitting two rows over in biology.
Who could forget eyes like those?
She should tell her that.
She should tell the woman right now.
Emma calls the woman's name,
but the woman has earphones in.
Her aviators wink like the automobile's hide.
The woman is nodding her head to the beat.
Smiling. The woman seems to know
the way to anywhere. Emma calls her name.
Once.
Twice.
Emma panics.

What if the woman does not hear her?
What if she drives away?
Emma sprints from her front seat to cross
the parking lot. Bends into the woman's open window,
Do.   You.   Remember.   Me?
The woman in the silver car says she does.
Removes her earphones
but does not remove her shades.
Emma only means to ask for directions.
But she cannot stop the lizards
busy knotting their tails in her gut
from leaping out of her mouth.
Even when the woman's smile turns mirage
the lizards tell the woman everything:
how this town is going to kill Emma,
how her boyfriend wants to marry her
if she can just get it together,
how her eyes aren't always pinpoints,
how much she could use a hug,
how much she loves her mother,
how much weight she lost in two weeks
feeling her way around the city's edges
for the exit sign out of here,
how the woman's face appears in the sun—
part flotation device, part angel. How she wants
to leave behind everyone and everything.
Everything in Emma's world could be dust,
if only the woman could just tell her which way
            is the right left.

Night on Rand Avenue

Two wasps copulate over your back porch—
their wings grate the air above the ochre splotch

where a hawk took down a pigeon last winter
not long after your move into the yellow house

with the purple door. The blood lingers, faint
against the painted brick as the condensation

of a fingerprint left on cold glass. After a year,
you've learned it doesn't matter what hour you step

on the porch to drink in the heady weight of lilac
from two doors down; people and strays stay steady

catching road. There. Two brothers carry a big-screen
away from a neighbor's house. There. Someone curses

at his friends half a block ahead to slow down.
You've learned who to not spare a word to.

Folks rarely look in your direction, nod, say hello.
You shift your weight, adjust the front of your shirt

to cover any hint of freckled breast. Children's voices
and a terrier's constant bark next door spill out

with the pools of light from your neighbor's kitchen.
A cop rolls by, hammerhead slow. Then another.

Someone was shot across the street last month—
gunshots here have their own sort of tongues.

You even fell asleep to their staccato pulse last New Year.
You stay here because you can afford it. But in your mind

you've already left behind your sinking bathroom,
the leak in the ceiling, cracks scrawled across two walls

and the mélange that lives nearby.
Just last night, a paraplegic woman hauled herself

up your steps and knocked on your storm door,
her motorized wheelchair left abandoned in the middle

of the street. Once, before you knew better, you wanted
desperately to put down roots in the thin soil here,

to strengthen your artist's bones against
the dense muscle of the 'hood in this yellow house

with the purple door across from the now empty lot
where Elizabeth Hardwick used to live. You fell in love

with the teal room, and the hardwood floors, and the church
choirs that compete each Sunday from either end of the street.

But the flickering streetlamps muddle the night, sheathe
each person and parked car in a translucent sepia haze.

Everyone you see is a haint. There. The boy with no shirt
who must stand to pedal on a too-large bike.

There. The men you can make out in the neighbor's yard
beyond billowing trap music and smoke from a grill.

There. Two wasps, although distracted for the moment,
may at any point be poised to sting. You make no loud noises.

No sudden movements. You retreat indoors.

the Quiet One

after "Bloodchild" by Octavia E. Butler

. . . it is one thing to read about dragons and another to meet them
—URSULA K. LE GUIN, *A WIZARD OF EARTHSEA*

When she first arrives you barely notice
the elevation in temperature,
because that could be anything,
maybe leftover steam-mist
from your shower
and not the benign smoke
from two armored nostrils.

If your eyes are old enough, a glimmer
of almost invisible iridescent scales
will catch the fluorescents when she shifts
her haunches to accommodate
your replacing the toilet paper roll
or a reach into the medicine cabinet
for eyedrops—there, when you close
the mirrored door you might glimpse
the flare of her opalescent eye,
accompanied by the scent of something
that reminds you pleasantly of burning leaves,
or, if she's in a foul mood, of burnt hair.

There used to be a time when a dragon
could appear in all her opulence
showing off the infernal nature
of her maw to thrill a body into submission.
If she fancied your build
and the way you said her name,

she might hypnotize you
until you slumbered standing upright.
She'd let you live so she could sow
her seed—her most vulnerable and most precious
thing—into your warm, soft belly for safekeeping.

Later, much later, she'd return, show up sudden
as midnight to a moonlit reveler,
open you up right there, in your sacral chakra's seam
and deliver an infant dragon tangled in your entrails
into the world, to enjoy its first fresh meal,
yet throbbing with the soursweet tang of life.

Now, the dragons have all outlived
the usefulness of their etymology.
They are so old, they have learned to hide
in the light so they may find a body
that doesn't tend to stray too far,
a body that likes to settle into its home
as though just beneath the plumbing
there lies buried a hidden horde of gold,
as familiar as bone.

She will wait for you first to notice her,
then to realize you've not mistaken a scale
or hooked tooth for shadow,
her veiny fabric of wing, curved talons,
and barbed tail for apparition or fatigue.
Because when you've finally, finally
seen her for what she is,
her whole hungry length snaking
from the plunger up to the shower-head,
a foreleg resting behind the faucet
nudging the hand soap against the toothpaste,
you will find you are unable to remember
a time when she was not always there.

Daughter of Nü Wa

—Common garter snake

The beheaded half of a *Thamnophis sirtalis* lays pale belly
up on the sidewalk in front of my home—no head or throat

anywhere in the grass or on the asphalt. Is this what's left
of the same slidebody I saw yesterday from the porch stoop

before the landscaper cut my lawn? He'd sheared
a serrated path with edge trimmers through the weeds

and grass alike, sparing no vegetation its bloom.
I had been sitting on this same feverish step, sweating

even from my ears. Hot sweat pooled, spilled over a lobe.
Then, movement. It was her, winding her ribboned

muscular length over the mulch. No fence, no glass slick
between us. She had been so careful, summoned by fingers

of warmth from beneath a canopy of indifferent earth
—a formal invitation to heat her blood—

the goddess looked away and back, away and back. Below the sky,
too far gone about its business of cascading into cloud and roof,

slithering down bark to notice either of us, she had stretched
out fully into the yard, without fear, into the sun.

Dead Blood

for Angel

Seen your boy the other day walkin'
with a white girl   as usual.
If I had known when I met him
he'd just end up wanderin' off
down the railroad tracks—
They whole family look the same.
They all got square heads, squat builds,
and funny-colored eyes that fade now
and then to the blond of new wheat.

    You remember

the one time we saw his mama
caterwaulin' on her front porch?
Crazy heifer.
She stay whorin'.
Told me if I didn't watch
my man she was going to bone
his brains out and take him from me.
I told *her*, Bitch, if you can pay
his bills too, you can have him.

    God,

what a waste.
Even blood can go to weeds.
Like that rash of kudzu in my backyard.

Pretty as a paycheck 'til it winds
around and through what you thought
was solid as a sycamore and then
one day you wake up   smothered.

    Don't you

think that boy and his kin should just—
I don't mean no harm,
but it's not like the world would even miss
them if they kindly did us all
the favor of dying out.

Hounded

The bitch

been followin' me for days from the house
like she gotta long-buried bone to pick.
They say she don't blink she so scared to
    let me out her sight.

Almost always she stay half a block behind,
tongue lollin', that nasty white spit caked
in the corners of her lips—she's turned
    into such a slobbermouth.

I close my eyes when she finally decides
to get close enough to leap and somethin'
guttural is born in us both. I keep my arm straight,
    just like he showed me.

The blade I been carryin' swivels from its bed
with a well-oiled snick—thirsty—and it's as if
she don't hear it or don't wanna see it comin',
    like her eyes are closed too.

And even when fat slug lines of somethin' dark
red and wet blooms from her muzzle, then from
her chest, I hold on until bone cracks, steel tongue
    lookin' for the letloose that will end

her.   And me.

Mulatta Muscle Memory

By the time you beat the black
into her she'll remember
nothing is thicker
than blood.

This Is Not a Self-Portrait

Here, in the cracked compact
mirror: one floating near-
sighted eye, briar
thatch of hair, overgrown
nostril, wayward
tooth, eyebrows
crawling to meet—
    rumors
of what lies unsettled
beneath the skin.

I'll come back as another woman

—TANYA TUCKER

On Falling

There's a dream that I believe / When I wake up, it goes away

—STURGILL SIMPSON, "I DON'T MIND"

It begins with the gray hour.
A downpour.
The dawn sun.
Walking trees.
    A caul of fog.
A slow procession—

A shadow sewn into a hem.

There are no fingerprints here.
There are no numbers.
    Only ceremony—a blizzard—
    blossoms falling over an orchard
    of upturned, veiled faces.
    Someone is a bride today.
    Someone's mouth will be empty of rice.
    Someone will be born an ancestor.
Hear this bell, a drum, a slow sweet wind,
a voice paddling through a lake

    that was once a grove of spirits,
    cut loose,
    wondering how
    anything could ever end.

First, there's a lasso,
and you're drowning.
No, first you're drowning,
then there's a lasso,
but I do not save you.
You are too heavy.
Instead.
I save a locket full of your hair
that's been bitten in half.
Now I have a tooth wandering
loose as a wraith in a hainthouse.
Then there's blood spilt
    from your palm.
I mark my forehead with it
    in a complex line.
        Paint it gold.
    I make a vow.   Break it.
There is a white tent in a desert of red.
Too much red.

You let go first.

For some reason
I don't mind.

I am young.
Too young to remember much
except falling for something
    bright in the water.
    Then there are hands.
Dark brown and big as wings.
        My mother's mouth floats
    above the wings, a vowel
            blurred by light.

Seconds rob me of my life.
I do not care.

        I am something new.
        The sky is a mirage.

My hair tangles in fronds
    growing beside me.

You crawl inside my shell.

A dream sets us
        adrift.

Witness

Yes, I'd seen him before.
He worked at the gas station
we all hate. The aisles feel
    claustrophobic
and there's not one time
we've been by where some guy
with a hand out and a sob story
about being broke down
and stranded hasn't asked us
for an absurdly specific amount
of change—eighty-seven cents,
a dollar forty-six, four nickels
and two pennies—to make a call,
catch the bus, or a cab home
to the other side of town.
Last time I was there
alone to buy two bottles of Ale-8
and he was working,
and I thought him handsome,
or maybe I thought about how
he might have been handsome once.
His name tag read *Lincoln*
and inky initials and icons
punctuated the skin on his fingers
and wrists and descended down
the neck of his uniform
into coarse, brown, curling hair,
and he managed to call me
sweetheart five times
in about thirty seconds,

but it sounded better than usual
in his baritone twang.
A thin scar slithered down
his chin, dividing the grizzle
of new beard. And though
he was in a hurry, he looked up
once from his register
and took the time to smile at me.
And he made me feel pretty.
And I pretended my bottles of Ale-8
were more interesting than his
hazel eyes. And I thought
how silly and stupid
I must be to care
what a gas station cashier
thinks of me. And how I'd forget
all about him as soon
as pedal hit road. But I would have
recognized him even from two-hundred feet
away on a downtown
city block when I was stopped
at a red light. And I did.
He was taking off his shirt
with a lit cigarette in his mouth,
practiced like, you know?
It was as if he didn't care
who saw him, as if he knew
the sun, for two seconds,
had turned his soft body
into a god's. And as he made
for the crosswalk,
he turned as though I'd called
him to face me.
I couldn't help myself.
I lifted my hand to wave,

at first like we were old friends
or country neighbors passing
one another down
a spaghetti-noodle of a two-lane road
but then, not in time, to tell him
to go back.   To stop.
          To wait.

thoughts you Can't take Back

I know you're married, but I've got feelings too

—MARTHA WAINWRIGHT

I find myself wondering how you kiss—what sort
of pressure you place on a woman's spine.
Do you pull her pelvis in, then press her back
against a wall? Do your hands wander,
lose themselves in the thin fabric of her blouse
and the supple swell of flesh above her fault line,
that low-slung denim waist? Do the fingers
of your right hand cradle her jaw while the fingers
of your left conjure a slow figure-eight lap of her hips?
Or do you, at her unspoken behest, invade—suggest
a more scenic route? Love, do you take the long way?
And what language do your lips choose to introduce
your tongues? Do you supplicate? Bow prostrate
before the sunrise that is her acquiescence? Do you lose
or keep track of time? And most important of all,
do you know when to let her up for air?

She Says to Him over Her Rim

You know,

> (here is where she drops
> her eyes artfully into topaz, swirls,
> inhales the bouquet of her _____)

you don't have to manhandle me—

> (here is where he splays lips,
> tongues teeth and releases
> his grip to show her his _____)

you already have my undivided attention.

> (they both glance below
> to where his fingers descend
> poised to slide between her _____)

All that Glitters

Her eyes do not change color when
he confesses he struck his woman once.
Maybe it's because she dug for it
and he admits this so plainly, without excuse.
Or maybe because they are still in bed,
and she is ensconced in plumes of purple silk.
They curve into bookends, hands drifting
over one another's feet and tomes of poetry.
In three years, he will still call her, *Lover*,
on the phone, will say he understands
why she needed to overturn the bookshelf,
how the wall asked for that hole,
why her dishes needed to hurl to the floor,
how her father's temper sprung sudden
from her temples like bright hoodoo pins,
why she dialed an old flame and not her mother.
His tongue will hum—ever a hive of bees,
Remember how you cracked open my
ribs and found what was lodged there?
She will say, *It certainly wasn't honey.*
He will say, *And yet, you keep coming*
back for more.

Alchemist

The woman next door says she don't
have to ask if it was me or him
rearranging the furniture last night.

Don't take that much to grow
a man the way you want him.

She tells me how all a woman
had to do to snag her the right man,
or cure one from being a terror
was to scare up some nightshade.

She says it used to be simpler
when the world was simpler.

Used to be in the South, you could
find it just about anywhere on account
of how liberal the law was with hanging men.

You'd look for the mandrake right where
he'd been hung and spasmed the last
of his seed into the earth.

But, she doesn't say, *spasmed his seed*.
She says something else which means
having an orgasm as you die.

You had to harvest the plant before dawn
on a Friday and you'd sometimes
get a four-foot root already bulging
into a homunculus.

But she doesn't say, *homunculus*.
She uses a racial slur.

Then it'd want feeding.
Goat's milk.
Honey.
Dried mushroom.
Blood from a fresh cut.

Eventually that little thing would come
to life, start moving around, wail
like an infant if it didn't have its food.

When it got adolescent-old
you'd slit its throatroot
because, after all, it's just a plant.

Dry it out.
Grind it down.
Serve it in tea to the man
you're wanting to do right and that was that.

What do you do now, I want to know,
if you don't have a mandrake?

She says, *Find someone who do.*
I know where a whole mess of 'em grow.

Antibiosis

By the time white hairs finally bloom
in his beard, he has stopped wearing
boxer briefs. Taken to wearing gym shorts
beneath his slacks. Reads love letters
from past lives with his tea leaves—
leaves them out tangled on his dresser
where he knows she will find them.
She notices for the first time his kisses
are too wet, his mouth opening as though
he were about to bite down to her pit.
One day, he comes home.
Finds her whittling a little man
out of driftwood with a steak knife.
When she is through, she soaks it in dishwater
pink with blood from so many little nicks.
Leaves it to dry by the succulents nesting
in terra cotta on the sill above the sink.
By the time spores lodge in its lap, turning
into a flourish of granite and jade lichen
that climbs from cock to core, she has gone
and stolen back what was left of herself,
having already loved him like his name
was etymological. Like she couldn't live
without him getting in under her skin.

Legend of the Boy and His Box

Watch what you say. The devil is listenin'.
He's got ears that you wouldn't believe

—THE BLACK KEYS, "THESE DAYS"

1 Once, a sad-mouthed woman happened upon
2 a boy (who was not really a boy) sitting
3 on the roots of a tree, surrounded by fallen fruit,
4 gazing into the day star. The woman wanted
5 him because his face was beautiful. She asked
6 that he stop staring at something so bright,
7 fearing his eyes would be bleached of color
8 or burn away. The woman picked him up
9 and gave him milk. And because he rarely spoke,
10 she told her secret, the only wish she'd ever had
11 for herself, to the boy (who was not really a boy).
12 And so, this is how he learned that other people
13 could long for more than their share, the way
14 he longed for more than his.
15 Because desire made them similar, the boy
16 (who was not really a boy) trusted the woman;
17 he opened his wicker box and let her listen
18 to all the voices he'd ever collected.
19 After they walked together for some seasons,
20 the woman found she had less of an urge
21 to fashion words about anything; she wondered
22 often why anyone ever spoke at all. The woman
23 forgot her secret, the only wish she'd ever had
24 for herself. Until, after she'd not said anything
25 for a very long time, the woman recognized
26 herself among his voices held in the wicker box.

27 She grew afraid—her voice stolen, wish forgotten—
28 the woman struck the boy (who was not really a boy).
29 He wandered again with a secret that did not belong
30 to him, his eyes a whole hue lighter
31 than they'd been the day before.

Ornithology Lesson

First thing we should do / if we see each other again is to make /
a cage of our bodies

—NICK FLYNN, "FORGETTING SOMETHING"

1.
You find me pirouetting slow
in a tent before an exaltation of men,
dim lights, the scent of refuse,
popcorn, and tobacco spit,
the clink of coins changing hands,
the lure of something both sordid
and sanctified.

2.
You follow me everywhere.
Where do you sleep?
I show you my thatch of straw.
What do you eat?
I serve you cave crickets and potato bugs.
How do you bathe?
I stand outside for an entire rain
leaping into puddles.
Why are the feathers at your throat red?
I say that is only for my mate to know.
How would your mate know?
My mate would not have to ask.

3.
Weary of your eyes,
I introduce you to Python Woman.

You mention her grip is impressive,
as is the overlapping leather of her scales,
but you find her endless bunching
and uncoiling unnerving. And the skins
all over her floor, leave you with night tremors.
Venom clings to every fiber.
It will take weeks to rid the rancid scent
of fear from your clothes.

4.
The first time you touch me is an accident.
We are laughing together,
as though you are not only interested
in my hollow bones or my tendency to molt
before I go onstage.
As though you would with anyone,
your hand reaches for me, eyes snapped
tight as two lids over mason mouths
your fingers graze a feather—halt
when they remember.

5.
I've seen you sitting mostly naked
patching together found feathers.
Are those supposed to be _____?

6.
The ringmaster wants you to leave.
The blood-coils around his eyes
convince you it is, in fact, time to go.
He sends the twins to watch you pack.
They argue over what kind of business
you might try that would be considered funny.

7.
You want to know the future.
Will I see you again?
Uncertain.
Do you feel anything for me?
I do not know.
Anything?
I tilt my head and do not blink. You hate that.
Then, good-bye.
I look to the sky, smell rain.

8.
Why I no longer fly:
From here, it is the same view.

Everyone is a fossil—
excavated marionettes breaking
through crests of earth.

From here, a collection of upturned
eyes is a light show splayed
over uncut stones.

Here, we are all seraphs caught
in a mist net, and left
abandoned by the sky.

A woman in the shape of a monster
a monster in the shape of a woman
the skies are full of them

—ADRIENNE RICH

I Would Make a Good Owl

The owl looked up to the stars above and sang to a small guitar
—EDWARD LEAR, "THE OWL AND THE PUSSYCAT"

If I could choose, I would be *Tyto alba*.
The barn owl.
I like the look of her face.

I think I could live in a tree.
A high, sweet pine.
Or in some cave nook.
Low light.
Plenty of bats.

Instead of arms, I imagine gilded wings
spread across the charcoal night.

Given the right nature,
I would kill
small, nesting, furred things—
pick their warm, trembling bodies off,
my fleshy talons holding them
with two-hundred times the grip
of the strongest man alive.

Each night, I would hunt, quiet as the moon,
returning to cough up collapsed bones
and pelts damp with digestion
into the mouths of my owlets.

I would be a good owl,
make my way through this world
on a song sung to stars.

Why I Do Not Write Poems about the Moon

The moon is nothing
but a great white carp
trapped in a dark tin of sky,
circled in on herself,
sucking her tail,
waiting to be fried.

She is a decanter
threatening to spill over,
drunk on her own ruddy spirit.
Swinging too low to the Earth,
she makes sloppy promises,
turns the tops of trees to rust.

One night she might ape
a blue specter's half-smile.
The next, a halo with its center
inked out by shadow.

Whatever her caper,
she proves a selfish player,
lingering at dawn,
well beyond her curtain call.

Uhura: On the Moon

Vulcan has no moon, Miss Uhura

—LIEUTENANT SPOCK

I was born during a dusk-storm.
The moment I stopped breathing
through water and tasted first, sweet
air, the rain ceased, and the moon moved
from behind two terrible clouds
to see herself in my face.
I've slept beneath her reflection,
her filmy fingers making a web
of the world, leaving me
the trapped star in its center.
I've made love beneath her
in an open field on a night that felt
like wading through cream.
I remember the first time I dreamt
of her up close—she was sheathed
in gold and gossamer damask.
I wanted to stick my tongue out
and lick her bloom—how did she
drift so? An amaryllis rooted
in the sky, elder sister to stars.

Guinan: On Listening

What I do is not listening.
It's more like picking out one voice
in the surround-sound of morning
through an open window.
Like hearing one birdcall at a time
and recognizing its owner,
or being able to tell one type
of engine over another by how
it accelerates through an intersection,
or which door is being opened and shut
somewhere in the house.
Blended together, it all sounds good—
the opening notes of a great number
to which we all know the words.
The difference between you and me
is that I may choose to focus
on the tambourine or the bass line
for an entire song.
The art of listening is an heirloom
I did not always understand.
El-Aurians take games such as
"Who Can Be Quiet the Longest?"
as seriously as a final exam.
You can imagine how exhilarating
our road trips must have been.
I remember my brother once bet me
I wouldn't be able to keep from
speaking for ten years.
For the first three, I scribbled notes
to everyone in a furious attempt to keep up
with conversations sidewinding around me.

I worried that if I wasn't being listened to,
I didn't matter.
I would be the only one
in the room no one noticed.
By the time I found my way into a voice again,
I figured out that if I sat still long enough,
someone would inevitably interject
what I had already thought to say.
It was as though the universe
was dialing everyone in a room
and leaving the same message.
It was as though we were all restating
the obvious, over and over again,
fumbling for meaning we already possessed.
They say I'm a good listener.
But this isn't listening.
This is just me, behind the bar,
mixing your voice in with a drink.

What the Alewife Knows

Beside the sea she lives, the woman of the vine, the maker of wine
— *EPIC OF GILGAMESH*

At the end of the world,
if you can catch Siduri
on the right midnight
    (better make it full
    moon bright
    with a peerless regiment
    of stardazzle),
after she has closed
the till, tucked up every loose
coin, sent each stray on his way,
if you make her laugh
at least once, offer her
an orchid for her hair;
if you promise her a song
in exchange
    (pray she loves
    your voice),
she will slip out
of her sandals, raise
an eyebrow, crook a finger,
lead you out through
the back door, and split
her hand-rolled with you.
Lifting her face into the salt-spray
of surf-striking-cliff, she will bid you
sip from her own gilded cask;
say nothing as she flexes
her toes into wet sand,

stares into the dark face
of sky, releases her hair
from its coils
    (but not her veil,
     not ever her veil),
and inhales rose smoke
before confessing how long
her vines have roped
their long selves around
in the soil, which of her fruit
grew tart in the sun
and which grew tender
in the shade of a broad leaf,
how many rains fell
last season, and how to tell
all of this from a single sip,
what vintage you serve kings
and what you serve paupers
    (it's not what you think),
and how here, at the end
of the world,
it is just the same
as the beginning:
the sum of a man
    (any man)
may be measured
by the potency of his draft.

Kamaishi Seashore Song

She is the only one who knows how to sing that song
—HIROYUKI MARUKI, *NEW YORK TIMES*, APRIL 5, 2011

It was my mother who taught me to sing.
But first, to run, carrying me on her back
away from the world's angry watermouth.
Then, I had no *shamisen*, no kimono,
and I knew only one lullaby by heart.
Now, I sing too many melodies
of riding into war. They weigh down
the back of my salvation. Year after year,
this hungry wet world wants more,
wants to dance the Miyako Odori,
wants to pluck me, wear me, wants
only an incense stick's worth of my time,
wants its own *mizuage*. Wants me
to remember its name. Wants everything
except to leave me alone.
The world leaves me next to nothing.
    My garments are gone.
    My instrument is gone.
    My home.
    My town.
    All gone.
Yet my hair remains.
My skin remains.
There is no mistaking this voice.
My lungs, full of exhaust, remain.

My spine is yet a willow's trunk.
My feet remember still the pulse of a planet.
This body knows much of the world, however wet.
Will always know when to sing.
Will always know when
              to run.

Jensu

after Vicissitudes *by Jason deCaires Taylor*

I am nothing but ash
drifting to the ocean floor

piling until rendered a proper shade.
I can already tell the light is different here.

I do not dare open my eyes.
I turn my head away, tighten

my hands around others' fearing saltpoison.
Eels slide across my shoulders.

My hair is heavier than the quiet.
When my teeth fall out, they do not grow back.

My ankles are a dwelling place for urchins,
my limbs, my torso, a canvas for scum.

Sometimes, the current brings rumors of life,
mimics voices, breeds memory.

I remember eating hot food.
I remember drinking milk.

I remember the sun before it turned
blue through my eyelids,

before a membrane of slow-moving
lips sealed my mouth, stopped my tongue.

How the Pythia Will Rot

after Priestess of Delphi, *John Collier (1891)*

The Sibyl, with frenzied mouth . . . yet reaches to a thousand years
with her voice by aid of the god

—HERACLITUS

Here, over a chasm
in the rock, she straddles
god's lip, the exhaust
of his pneuma.
So near the navel
of the world, her groin
condenses with his vapor
and she remembers how
just last year,
her belly rose—perfect orb
great with child,
torso swelling into the sun,
tempting a celestial gaze.
Now, the world is a blur
of light, a shallow basin
of cool water, a fistful
of laurel leaves,
sheer red silk,
and the company of naiads.
Lips moving constantly,
her tongue gropes between
them for a ceiling beyond
the roof of this cavern,
beyond
      beyond.

Simbi

In my black, sequined pocketbook,
a brushed-metal mermaid with golden hair
pins an index card to an old movie ticket stub.

17

She has only ever possessed half
of a left hand. She is ashamed of it.
Keeps it tucked under her chin as she guards
my library card and loose change.

17 8

Crumbs of loose-leaf tobacco
and dried flower petals brush against
her clavicle smelling of subterranean charms.
She would dive to them if she could, but then,
she must be the only waterwoman
in the world who never learned to swim.

17 8 64

She is intimately acquainted
with my driver's license photo
and other frayed ephemera.
Can recite what's written
on a lipstick-smudged yellowing
fortune-cookie fortune like it is poetry:

*The skills you have gathered
will one day come in handy.*

17 8 64 32

With cool, broken knuckles fixed
always against her chin,
she contemplates this.
How living thus, in the sateen dark
will one day reveal its handiness.

17 8 64 32 5

On the back of the fortune
are numbers.
She counts on them
to keep time
more accurately
than my cellular clock.

17 8 64 32 5, 9

This way she can track
the pocketbook's open-and-shut,
her every dawn and dusk:

17 8 64 32 5, 9
9 17 8 64 32, 5
5 9 17 8 64, 32
32 5 9 17 8, 64
64 32 5 9 17, 8
8 64 32 5 9, 17

She waits for her turn to resurface.

17

Remains
        waiting.

Field Notes from Oz: An Excerpt

> I don't want these shoes . . .
>
> —DOROTHY, *THE WIZ*

Some days I feel like a real Diana,
and the ease is easy—
comes no matter how far
we've got left to go.
I revolve into a cyclone
of arms and afro
and my smile is brighter
than the fractured
reflection of a disco ball.
Other times, these silver stilettos
moving staccato across painted
brick remind me too much
of the fairy tale I tell
my students back home
to scare them
into being sweet—you know
the one about the little girl
who danced her feet down
to bone 'cause she thought
she was too cute
in her fancy red shoes.
Most days, I can barely remember
how to tell time by the sun—
can't remember a time
when the world wasn't
a mirage of emeralds—
can't remember the last time
I smelled anything

but straw and oil and dander
and the lingering scent
of that cheap champagne
them Poppy Girls call perfume.
I tried to tell that ol' mystic
bag lady I didn't want these
dead woman's shoes.
Only place they've eased me
down so far is farther away
from home.

If thou openest not the gate to let me enter,
I will break the door. I will wrench the lock.
I will smash the door-posts. I will force the doors.
I will bring up the dead to eat the living
and the dead will outnumber the living.

—*EPIC OF GILGAMESH*, "DESCENT OF THE
GODDESS ISHTAR INTO THE LOWER WORLD"

Dream State

Even in her sleep
she stays ready to spring away
from monsters and men.

Dark Moon

...she built a roaring fire, then doubled up the body ... and pushed it into the flames. Through the night she tended the fire as it consumed the mortal remains of her former master

—MELTON A. McLAURIN, *CELIA, A SLAVE*

I prefers it this way, alone in the dark,
as used to fear as I am. Fear is good.
Fear mean I'se still alive.

And I feels a kind of kinship with the lonely,
low-hangin' moon, now as swole as my own
pregnant belly. After all, the moon taught me

how to stay hid out in the open. And the moon
ain't never not the moon. Even behind
the almighty sun, she there, faint as chalk.

Anyhow, I'se used to feelin' fear durin' a stretch
of dark moon. Thems were his favorite nights
to visit. I learnt to spect to see him old as he was,

creepin' 'round horny as a boy just learnin' to fiddle
with himself. And here he come crossin' the yard
to my hut like I'se some dumb sheep in a field.

George and the others scared to say his name
out loud but I names him the demon he is.
Plain sight. Now we gon' hide in plain sight.

I stays up all night with one eye on my sleepin'
chilren, and one on the fireplace. I stokes
the wood all 'round his soft, white body,

and I watches it bubble up then char, tongues
of flame remindin' me too much of his own
across my flesh. I keeps watch—

cold as the dark moon—lets myself burn
with him for the last time down to ash.
Down to bone.

Lynching Postcard

after Laura Nelson

You can stretch my neck on that old river bridge
—WOODY GUTHRIE, "DON'T KILL MY BABY AND MY SON"

I want to imagine there is no rope hankering
for a brownwoman's throat and the asterism
that was her voice. Next, that her arches rest
on something as firm yet giving as loam.
And there is no faceless mob. No ambivalent
tree line. No sepia stream below. No proverbs.
No promised land—My God—what is left
for her but an absence of light? Whose ancestor
could she possibly be now? I want to reach
for her ring-finger hand. I want to tidy her hair.
Button her sleeves. Smooth the wrinkles from
her dress. Set the angle of her head back to where
her spine has not yet given way to the pressure
of hand-rolled hemp and gravity's blurred desire.
I want to open her eyes. Tell her one-hundred
years later that she should have been born a gust
of cobalt, a blue ember against the granite
swathe of sky, that she hangs on still as more
than a souvenir.

Beyond the Bridge: A Lynched Woman Speaks

You wait in line 'long
with everyone else,
and what a body wore
as flesh when they was alive
don't matter in the line.
Take me—a black gal
from Kentucky with bare feet
and somethin' strung 'round
her neck that won't fall
off, not even in death,
could be ahead of someone
important like a general.
Dead folks don't talk much.
Only thing on our mind
is the last thought
we had before we died:
our kinfolk, the window
we left open on accident,
our favorite color of sky,
how we never imagined
we'd die in the dirt.
No matter what you ask
us, to make conversation,
we'd just say somethin'
that don't match, like,
I coulda' given Miriam
that extra spoonful
of molasses last week
on her biscuit.

And that's the main thought
that stay with us always.
But mostly we just standin'
in line tryna 'member
other little details like how
one kinda' fabric feel different
from another.
You know, that it's burlap,
not silk that's rough.
At the front of the line,
everyone get handed
they own piece of luggage.
Inside, little objects
from over your whole life
add up to clues
to wherever you
'posedta go next:
Piece of patchwork
from your mama's quilt.
Spray of flowers
from your beau.
Coupla' bobby pins.
Framed portrait
with the cracked glass.
Mother-a-pearl cufflink
you thought you'd lost.
Letter you never mailed
to your sister.
If you can piece it
all together, all them little
shards you never
thought to pay much
mind to or forgot to notice,
if you can figure
what the world
was tryna' tell you all 'long,

you get to move on to
whatever come next.
Only problem is,
you been waitin' in line
forgettin' just about everythin'
you ever did know.
So you gotta head back
the way you come,
start nosin' 'round
for clues from the livin'.
But it mighta' been five
years or five-hundred
since you been back.
Things move around so fast
when you get outta' line.
Kinfolk gone,
moved on,
or dead.
House sold
or knocked down
for somethin' new.
Streets change.
Land dips
where it used'ta dive.
Honey, even the stars'll burn
out if you wait long enough.
Sometimes,
when you get a little shiver
for no real reason,
a rash of gooseflesh
like someone run a new leaf
'tween your shoulder blades,
don't worry none.
It's just one of us
wayfarin' haints,
shufflin' 'round, waitin'

for somethin' that'll lead
us to whatever bridge
will let us cross to anywhere
but from where
we already been.

Zulaikha: On Fire

He always sends his zombies in first—
zombies don't blink, clumsy hands
batting out flaming curtains to get to her.
They do not make a sound, even as their gray,
pocked skin peels back from rotted muscle
in the face of her little inferno.

What a lovely way to burn

She is always sitting in the same place:
center of the living room, rocking hard enough
to uproot in a wicker chair over a braided rug,
watching her four terra-cotta walls flake away.
A midnight hand finds her, steers her outdoors.
No use to struggle.
This is all routine.
What's left of her home is char anyway.

What a lovely way to burn

The lawn is soot.
The fence, now ash, floats down to the soot,
still something of a whitewashed perimeter.
Her captor is wearing a fireproof uniform.
What were you thinking! his three heads shout.
She says nothing. His many eyes have no pupils.

What a lovely way to burn

They watch the smoke eddy above
the shingles, smudging a too-large, dull, red sun.

A dying sun. He has been ordered to confiscate
her torches. Her twigs. Her beeswax candles.
Even her flint. His orders will leave her alone
in the barbarous dark.

What a lovely way to burn

He hefts a hose, turns the water on, and she dreams
she is a beauty again, can still enjoy a rush
of crisp water and not tremble so hard
that she breaks bones. The dream turns
the rivets in her palms and knuckles
into lines of henna, dissolves the scars
webbing her fingers, and fastens
brilliant scarabs into newly grown hair.

What a lovely way to burn

A mirage chips the overlapping scales away
from her torso and limbs—no longer does she appear kin
to the dragons her brothers used to track through caves.
No more blisters seep fluid into her eyes.
This way with her home ablaze, she can still dream
that she remembers what it means to know warmth.

Palimpsest: The Lynched Woman Continues

In Next Place,
you get you a new hide.
But first, you got to turn
in the old.
You get led
to this little room barely bigger
than a water closet with nothin'
but a hook on the wall
that got your new hide hangin' up
waitin' on you.
And there's no chair,
no table, no cot.
Nothin' a body needs
to make itself at home.
If it's too dark in there,
you think:
light
an' just like that
things get brighter
even without a window
or a lamp.
Too cool, you think:
warm
an' then the gooseflesh goes
away but there's no fire,
no pot-bellied stove.
You cain't help but smile
an' get happy,
like maybe this a sign
of things to come.

An' at this point
you ain't sure of much
but one thing—
somehow you got
to find a way
to get out of your old skin.
Somehow you got to
make like a cicada
and leave behind
what you was born into,
stretched out,
an' walked around in
alla' your last life
an' part of this one.
An' that's when
it really sets in
what you got to do,
an' you start to panic.
It took you all this time
to get to know
who you was
an' what's expected of you.
You cain't see
how to let alla' that go.
You don't want no new hide
you got to break
in all over again.
You got it wrong.
You don't wanna be in
Next Place no more.
You'd rather wander
the earth with alla'
your scars 'n bruises
an' close calls right where
they 'posedta be:
on the outside.

You earned 'em,
a lifetime
of open-'n-shut wounds—
without 'em
to remind what you done
been through,
who are you?
Who you be?
Ain't no doors
so you beat on the walls.
Ain't no way out but in.
Ain't nothin' to throw.
Ain't nothin' to break
but your own skin.
So you do.
Just a fingernail's worth
is all it takes at first
before you start
to unravel at the seams,
but you barely notice
you so busy scrapin' away
what you did
the first time
he broke your heart,
what you did
when she left for good,
what you didn't say
but shoulda',
what you did say
but should'na,
the times you fell
with somebody to catch you,
the times you leapt
when you knew no one would,
until you standin' there
like a birch tree, limbs

almost all peeled apart.
An' all you got to do then
is shrug that old hide off,
step out an' away an' leave
what's left of someone
you usedta' know
in a heap a rottin' scraps
on the floor.
By that point a new hide
don't sound so bad.
When you go
to pick it up offa' that hook
you think it'll be heavy
but it's light,
you think it'll be cold
but it's warm,
you turn it over an' over
in your hands
tryna' figure what the new you
'posedta look like, an' that's when
you notice the linin'.
You know how on one
of them 'spensive coats
rich folks get tailor made
from somewhere outta town
like New York City or Paris,
there's always this satin
or silk linin' sewn in,
an' the coat so fine,
you cain't help
but wonder
how somebody like you
can afford to dream
about let alone ever try
on or buy?
Yeah, it's like that.

An' you can barely believe
this meant for poor ol'
ruined, scared, and tremblin' you.
But the linin'—
alla' them scars you just tore
offa' your outsides
is pressed into the insides
of this new hide real neat
and precise like.
An' there are more than
you remember,
more from the last time
you was in this room.
An' the time before that.
An' the time before that.
An' a hundred times before that.
An' they just layered
an' pressed all over
one another like layers
of thin gauze or paper
you can see all
the way through.
An' that's when you know—

Call Her by Her Name

↳ referrence to Zulaikha

Not your Prologue.
Not your Open Road.
Not your Trophy.
Not your Icing-on-the-Cake.
Not your Pacifier.
Not your High-Noon.
Not your Alibi.
Not your Rung.
Not your Slur.

Not your Wormhole.
Not your Ingrown Hair.
Not your Fool's Errand.
Not your Excuse.

Not your Infinite Loop.
Not your Succubus.

Not your Nightmare.
Not your Anecdote.
Not your Microcosm.
Not your Exhibition.
Not your Demon.

Not your Zeitgeist.
Not your Umbilical Cord.
Not your Lust.
Not your Abomination.
Not your Icon.
Not your Kingdom come.

Not your High-Horse.
Not your Affliction.

Not your Whitewash.
Not your H-Bomb.
Not your Inheritance.
Not your Cause-and-Effect.
Not your Hired Hand.

Not your Mother.
Not your Event Horizon.
Not your Absent Mind.
Not your Narcotic.
Not your Scapegoat.

Not your Boiling Point.
Not your Republic.
Not your Idol.
Not your Life Jacket.
Not your Limited Edition.
Not your Inner City.
Not your Answer.
Not your Non Sequitur.
Not your Taboo.

Not your Bottom Line.
Not your Echo Chamber.
Not your Abstraction.
Not your Universe.
Not your Toilet Bowl.
Not your Yo-Yo.

Not your Narrow Escape.
Not your Opus.
Not your Talisman.

Not your Phantom Limb.
Not your Entrée.
Not your Reprieve.
Not your Jacob's Ladder.
Not your Underworld.
Not your Rabbit Hole.
Not your Epithet.
Not your Resolution.

What Women Are Made Of

There are many kinds of open

—AUDRE LORDE, "COAL"

We are all ventricle, spine, lung, larynx, and gut.
Clavicle and nape, what lies forked in an open palm;

we are follicle and temple. We are ankle, arch,
sole. Pore and rib, pelvis and root,

and tongue. We are wishbone and gland and molar
and lobe. We are hippocampus and exposed nerve

and cornea. Areola, pigment, melanin, and nails.
Varicose. Cellulite. Divining rod. Sinew and tissue,

saliva and silt. We are blood and salt, clay and aquifer.
We are breath and flame and stratosphere. Palimpsest

and bibelot and cloisonné fine lines. Marigold, hydrangea,
and dimple. Nightlight, satellite, and stubble. We are

pinnacle, plummet, dark circles and dark matter.
A constellation of freckles and specters and miracles

and lashes. Both bent and erect, we are all give
and give back. We are volta and girder. Make an incision

in our nectary and Painted Ladies sail forth, riding the back
of a warm wind, plumed with love and things like love.

Crack us down to the marrow and you may find us full
of cicada husks and sand dollars and salted maple-taffy

weary of welding together our daydreams. All sweet tea,
razor blades, carbon, and patchwork quilts of *Good God!*

and *Lord Have Mercy!* Our hands remember how to turn
the earth before we do. Our intestinal fortitude? Cumulonimbus

streaked with saffron light. Our foundation? Not in our limbs
or hips; this comes first as an amen, a hallelujah, a suckling,

swaddled psalm sung at the cosmos' breast. You want to
know what women are made of? Open wide and find out.

Thanks to my family: my mother, Glenna, my father Ron, and my little sister Veronica, who remain excellent stewards of my confidence.

Thanks to Frank X Walker for the ark that is his heart.

Thanks to Nikky Finney for the compass that is her voice.

Special thanks to the following folks for laying eyes and hands on this collection first:

Hendrick Floyd for constantly challenging me to push the envelope. Rebecca Gayle Howell for her surgeon's precision. David Cazden who teaches me something new every time. Katerina Stoykova-Klemer for her nurturing guidance. E. C. Belli for her openness and enthusiasm. Jeremy Paden, whose compassionate critiques should win him an award for most-suffered-through first drafts.

My deepest gratitude to Parneshia, Gianna, and the wonderful team at Northwestern University Press (Nathan, Marianne, Greta, and Laura) for midwifing me and my work through this process.

A special shout-out to my collaborators, artists, and arts enthusiasts of the most supreme caliber with whom I hope to always ask, "What if?": Angel Clark, Kate Hadfield, Jami and Brandy Shumake-Young, LeTonia Jones and the SwallowTale Project crew, Ellie Clark, Landon Antonetti, Rachel Bryant, Elizabeth Beck, Paul Michael Brown, Michelle Hollis, Justin Long, Willie Eames, David Farris, Caleb Ritchie, Art Mize, Mason Colby, Marcus Wilkerson, Jeremiah Muwanga, Duane Lundy, Kremena Todorova, Kurt Gohde, Andrea Fisher, Brian Campbell, Neil Chethik and the staff of the Carnegie Center for Literacy and Learning, Cave Canem, and my first artistic family, the Affrilachian Poets.

Thanks to the following publications where versions of these poems have previously appeared:

"Jengu": *LaFovea*

"This Is Not a Self-Portrait": *Bigger Than They Appear: Anthology of Very Short Poems* (Accents Publishing)

"Legend of the Boy and His Box," "Kamaishi Seashore Song," "Simbi," and "How the Pythia Will Rot": *Conclave Journal*

"Lynching Postcard" and "Beyond the Bridge: A Lynched Woman Speaks":
   The Journal of Feminist Studies in Religion

"Dead Blood": *Drunken Boat*

"Hounded": *Duende*

"All That Glitters": *Muzzle*

"Why I Do Not Write Poems about the Moon": *The Louisville Review*

"Zulaikha: On Fire," "Antibiosis," and "The Other Left": *Rabbit Catastrophe Review*

"Ornithology Lesson": The Red Room; *TheThe Poetry Collection*

"She Says to Him over Her Rim": *Small Batch Anthology* (Two of Cups Press)

"Daughter of Nü Wa" and "Alchemist": *Still: The Journal*

"What the Alewife Knows" and "What Women Are Made Of": *Verse Wisconsin*

"On Falling": *White Space Poetry Anthology*

"Night on Rand Avenue": *Oxford American*

"Pedicure": *Wingbeats* (Dos Gatos Press)

"Recess: A Bop": Lyrics are from "Shimmy Shimmy Ko-Ko-Bop," written by Bob Smith and performed by Little Anthony and the Imperials in 1959.

"Daughter of Nü Wa": Nü Wa is best known as the Chinese deity responsible for creating people. She is most often depicted as having the head of a woman and the body of a serpent.

"Kamaishi Seashore Song": The eighty-four-year-old Tsuyako Ito has been a geisha since she was fourteen. She has survived four tsunamis. A *shamisen* is a three-stringed musical instrument similar to a guitar or banjo. Miyako Odori is a traditional geisha dance event. *Mizuage* means "hoisting from the waters." In this context, I am using it to refer to the coming of age ceremony for an apprentice geisha.

"Jengu": A *jengu* is a Cameroonian water spirit with long wooly hair and gapped teeth.

"Simbi": A *simbi* is a Haitian water-serpent spirit, in Vodou a *lwa* (spirit) of plants and leaves sometimes associated with transporting messages and souls, known as the "twice-born ancestor."

"Dark Moon": On the night of Saturday, June 23, 1855, a slave named Celia—in order to counter the sexual abuse she'd endured since her early teenage years, as well as to appease a jealous lover, George, her fellow bondsmen—bludgeoned to death her master, Robert Newsom, before burning his body in her fireplace and burying what was left of his bones beneath her house and scattering his ashes throughout the yard.

"Lynching Postcard": Laura Nelson and her teenage son, L. D. Nelson, were lynched on May 25, 1911, from a bridge near Okemah, Oklahoma, over the North Canadian River, after being charged with the murder of a sheriff. Photographs of the bodies were sold as postcards. Laura's photo is the only known photo of a female lynching victim.

"Zulaikha: On Fire": Zulaikha is known popularly as "Potiphar's wife" in the Old Testament. Dante's *Inferno* portrays her as suffering in the eighth circle of Hell from a burning fever for committing the sin of perjury.